Four Pairs of Shoes

Ian Baltutis

ISBN 13: 978-1975987619
ISBN 10: 1975987616

Table of Contents

Answering the Call to Leadership

"You have to take risks. We will only understand the miracle of life fully when we allow the unexpected to happen."

Nathan Coelho

In June 2013, while on family vacation with my parents, brother, and fiancée, I got a phone call from a close friend from undergrad. She was working as a reporter in Burlington, NC, where we'd both stayed after graduation from Elon University in 2008. Her latest assignment was covering local government for the weekly newspaper, and she asked if I'd been following who was filing to run for City Council in the upcoming election. I replied that I hadn't, and admitted that politics wasn't something that particularly interested me. I'd volunteered a few times for the local Obama campaign in 2012, during which I'd spent a night making phone calls and a couple Saturdays knocking doors, but that was the extent of my political involvement.

"Would you consider running for City Council?" she asked. "All the incumbents have filed for re-election, but the slate of challengers is very limited. People are pretty tired of status quo politics, so I think you'd have a good chance of winning one of the Council seats."

If anyone else had made the pitch, I probably would have just laughed it off and politely declined. But Lesley and I had been friends for a long time, and I trusted her opinion. Perhaps I was a little flattered that she thought I would be good at the role. I thanked her for the suggestion and said I'd consider it.

Throughout the rest of the day, my mind wandered again and again to the idea of City Council. I moved to North Carolina from Minnesota for college, and although I'd lived there for nearly seven years, it didn't completely feel like home yet. However, I'd founded a product design business in town and was actively working on opening a brewery as well. My entrepreneurial mind saw opportunity in every situation, and Burlington was no exception. What could Burlington be with the right leadership? Could it be transformed from a quiet southern town where students counted down the days until they left to a vibrant community where people couldn't wait to move back? The more I thought, the more excited I became about the possibilities.

Looking through the limited information available online, I found that the process of filing to run for City Council was the same as the process of filing to run for Mayor. Furthermore, I realized that, although the City Council race was already moderately contested, the mayoral race wasn't. The incumbent Mayor was running for re-election to a fourth term, and he had run functionally unopposed during several of his past elections. Could I challenge him? At the very least, if I ran against him, his actions during his past three terms, or lack thereof, would be called into question. Certainly that would draw more attention to the election than if I was one in the crowd of City Council hopefuls. Even if all I accomplished was more voter engagement and more constructive conversations about the future of the city, that would be a success.

I pitched the idea to my fiancée, Kristina. She was cautiously supportive, and I suspect she understood the magnitude of the undertaking better than I did. She would later tell me that, had our roles been reversed, she wouldn't have wanted me to deny her the opportunity, so she couldn't in good conscience deny me the opportunity in this case. I barely got any sleep that night as thoughts raced through my head.

As I mentioned, Kristina and I were on family vacation with my parents and brother while all of this happened. We had flown from North Carolina to Minneapolis, MN, where my family still lives, and caught the westbound Amtrak Empire Builder train to Portland, Oregon, where my aunt and uncle live. This is how my family vacationed during my childhood, and I had fond memories of waking up early, waiting at the train station, loading our luggage on board, settling in to the family room of the sleeper car, wandering up and down the rocking train compartments, taking terrible blurred photos of landscapes flying by at 80mph, and falling asleep to the clickity-clack and gentle swaying of the train. It had been over a decade since our last family trip, but sharing these stories with Kristina early in our relationship had sparked a desire to relive the experience. Consequently, not long after our engagement, I'd pitched the idea that we organize a family trip, just like the ones from when I was younger.

We had arrived in Portland a few days earlier, and our plan for the day was to drive down to Astoria after breakfast. Although searching online for information about how to file for office yielded few results, I did discover that the filing deadline was the next day. In a panic, I called the Alamance County Board of Elections to seek their guidance. Initially, they recommended that I just come down to their office, since that was the easiest way to file, and asked if I needed directions. When I replied that I was in Portland, Oregon and therefore would not be able to drive down to the office, they were dumbfounded. I had downloaded the necessary forms from their website, but they required the signature of a notary public. I asked if the notary public had to be from North Carolina, or if an Oregon notary public would do. They had no idea, since no one had ever asked. They said they would consider it and call back. Thus began a game of phone tag between the Alamance County Board of Elections, the North Carolina State Board of Elections, and myself while we attempted to sort out all that would be necessary for me to file for office from the other side of the country. My family loaded the car for the trek to Astoria and waited not-so-patiently for me to sort out the details.

After printing the forms, we hit the road. Sitting in the second-row-middle-seat (there being a bit more legroom for my 6' 6" lanky self in the middle), I began filling in the forms. We would need to have them notarized and overnighted, and I'd found a UPS Store along the route, just across the border in Longview, WA, to serve that purpose. When we arrived and explained what we needed, they informed me that to notarize the forms I would need to complete them in their presence. Our trip to Astoria experienced yet another slight delay while we reprinted the forms, completed them again, I checked the box for "Mayor" one more time, took a photo to document the moment, sealed the envelope, and overnighted the forms back to North Carolina.

Looking back now, I had no idea what I had just done. But for the moment, we turned back to our family vacation. By the following afternoon, it hit the press in Burlington that some relatively unknown kid who wasn't even from around here was challenging the six-year incumbent Mayor. My phone started ringing with requests for interviews. I stalled answering those phone calls at first, unsure of how I would answer if someone asked about my platform or my vision for the city. I'd never studied political science, I'd never run a campaign, and I'd never even been to a City Council meeting. I believe this ultimately worked to my advantage - not knowing how I was "supposed to" do it freed me from those obligations and allowed me to approach campaigning in a new and innovative way.

I knew that I wanted relationships and citizen engagement to be the driving force of my campaign. Even though I ultimately lost that election in 2013, voter turnout increased 50% over historical off-year mayoral elections, and since my goal for that campaign was to increase citizen engagement, I like to consider that election a success. But I knew that I still had more to offer. I ran for NC State House District 63 in 2014 and lost again, but still didn't give up. Finally, in 2015, using the same approach I had used the two years prior - one-on-one conversations, door-to-door introductions, I won the mayoral seat.

My mission has always been about meeting people at their doorstep and having honest conversations about their dreams for the future of Burlington. It is my hope that this book will offer a look behind the scenes at my journey to become the youngest mayor in Burlington's history, as well as share my vision for the future we can only accomplish together.

One Step at a Time

"Lowly, unpurposeful, and random as they may appear, sidewalk contacts are the small change from which a city's wealth of public life may grow."

Jane Jacobs

Writing a campaign platform from scratch, while having never attended a City Council meeting, was an exercise in creativity. Fortunately, in those first few weeks, the press was mostly interested in biographical questions. Those were easy since, as an entrepreneur, I'd perfected my 60-second elevator pitch and was skilled at telling my story at the drop of a hat. For responses to policy questions, however, I had a lot to learn. Kristina and I crafted some concepts for focusing on innovation and community-sourced ideas. We wanted to build a community with a clear vision of its goals and emphasize a local government that had a personal relationship with its constituents and understood their challenges.

The night before Kristina and I left Portland, we went out for dinner with my aunt and uncle. Over a few rounds of Portland craft beer at a sidewalk cafe on Alberta St, we brainstormed a campaign slogan and brand. Our slogan was "Community Builds Community" and it featured a logo depicting people, a house, and a small business storefront with arrows connecting them to each other, similar to the recycling symbol. Our campaign would be about engaging the people of Burlington to take a more active role in defining the future of their city.

A week or so after filing, I was back in Minnesota and was helping my mother with the restoration of a 1912 Craftsman house in Mound, MN. I had taken a break from repairing 100-year-old plaster and was enjoying a chance to rest my feet and eat a medium thin crust pizza. As I sat covered in plaster dust, enjoying a rejuvenating flood of sunlight from the large dining room windows, my phone rang. I had reached out to enlist help from people who knew what was involved in political campaigns, and the first of those people was a fellow Elon alumnus named Garrett. He'd graduated a few years before me and we met during our time on Elon University's Young Alumni Council. Garrett is a politics junkie with a golfing habit. He can spend endless hours telling stories about either. He'd started in politics crisscrossing North Carolina working for Lieutenant Governor Walter Dalton in his bid for the Governor's race in 2012. Garrett was born and raised in the state, so he knew the history of Carolina-style politics and was excited to help me prepare for what was ahead.

Garrett and I talked through my hopes for the scale and scope of my campaign. Terms like constituent groups, win-number, grassroots campaigning, and canvassing would not become a regular part of my vocabulary until much later, but Garrett eased me into the concepts. Burlington was one of the larger cities in North Carolina with around 51,000 residents at that time. Thanks to several less-than-exciting past municipal elections, coupled with the inherent voter apathy for off-year elections, turnout was usually just a few thousand voters for elections like mine.

"The strongest campaigns are those where you knock doors," Garrett explained. "And I can pretty much guarantee you that an incumbent opponent isn't going to the put in the time to walk neighborhoods. How do you feel about knocking some doors?" At the time, I had no idea that by "some," Garrett meant a few thousand, but it sounded like an appealing idea. I could picture myself exploring the city, walking through quiet neighborhoods on pleasant sunny days and cheerfully introducing myself to the voters of Burlington. My vision might as well have included small woodland creatures helping me along as we strolled the city and hummed a happy tune. Garrett assured me it would be very straight forward. We'd pull the list of all the people who had voted in at least 2 of the 3 previous mayoral elections, and all I had to do was meet all of them and ask for their vote. It sounded easy enough, and it fit perfectly with my community-oriented, fledgling campaign platform, so I readily agreed.

Over the next three and a half months, I would walk 132 miles, knocking on 4,283 doors, and talking to thousands of people. In total over my three campaigns, I have walked hundreds of miles, knocking on over 12,000 doors, and created many wonderful memories along the way. I was usually greeted cautiously but politely. Sometimes those interactions melted into pleasant conversations in living rooms and front porches, often accompanied by a glass of iced water or sweet tea. I continued my door-to-door march regardless of the weather, and I found that the best weather for canvassing is a light, misting rain. It's significantly cooler, and people are more willing to listen to someone who is so dedicated to their message that they don't pack up and seek shelter at the first sign of less-than-ideal conditions. Thank you all those who offered me brief respite from the pounding rain and blazing sun along the way.

All this walking has ruined a few pairs of shoes, but in their own way, these shoes tell a story. Their change in style reflects the evolution of myself as a candidate. Their battered soles reflect my commitment to the goal of meeting people where they are, rather than waiting for them to come to me. They have been there with me as I listened to stories of hope, worry, defeat, and second chances. These are the same stories which I use to inform my decisions as Mayor and which I mold into the scaffolding of our community initiatives. Their story is my story, and I'm honored to share that story here.

Old Enough to Vote

*"Leaders must wake people out of inertia. They must get
people excited about something they've never seen before,
something that does not yet exist."*

Rosabeth Moss Kanter

I've always been told that I look younger than I am, but
that was never a problem until I started knocking doors as
a mayoral candidate. The comments started from day one.
I'd walk up to the front door of a house, ring the bell, and
after a few moments someone old enough to be my parent,
or grandparent, would open the door and peer at me
quizzically. I would launch into my introduction.

"Good morning/afternoon/evening, my name is Ian
Baltutis and I am here because I am a candidate running
for Mayor of the City of Burlington. I was wondering if you
had a few minutes to share what issues are important to
you this election year."

At this point I usually got one of two responses. First,
"What did you say your name was?" Second, "You don't
look like you're old enough to vote."

I laughed it off, every time. I'd press on, saying, "I get that a lot. I'm actually 27 years old and I'm here because I believe that politics should be personal. I wanted to take the time to personally meet you and ask for your vote." At this point, it would start to sink in that they were face-to-face with a truly grassroots candidate, the likes of whom they had never seen on their doorstep. Usually the conversation would then turn away from my age and I finally got to learn more about the people I was visiting - their story, their interests, their hopes for the community.

The comment was still something I dreaded. While I could get past it relatively quickly, I still tried my best to prevent it in the first place. To try to look older, I dressed in a full suit, tie, and dress shoes. Walking outside into the hot, thick air of North Carolina in August, sweat would instantly gather on my brow. If there is a suit that is good for this weather, I didn't find it.

I'd start knocking doors in the early afternoon. Dressed up, I'd drive to a neighborhood and park. I'd climb out of my little green hatchback with my clipboard and a stack of campaign flyers, then start walking. Within a house or two, my undershirt was damp and sticky. As I walked between houses, I'd claw at my shirt to keep it looking neat and pull the bunched fabric from my armpits. As I turned to walk up to the next house, I'd pause, collect my thoughts, and then march up to the door, knowing that despite this The Comment would still come.

The black dress shoes I wore with this getup were nothing special, just a pair of store-brand shoes I'd had since high school and which had been worn no more than a few dozen times. They had never been polished, as their original shine had never worn off, but that would soon change. By the end of that first month, those shoes had pounded over fifty miles. The toes had been scuffed over countless brick steps and rough pavement. Slashes and gouges marked them such that no amount of polish would ever bring back their luster. However, what I did to the shoes was nothing compared to what they did to my feet.

The last day I ever wore those shoes, I was canvassing near Davis Street West. At that time, I would park the car in one spot, then get out and canvas two or three blocks out, one door at a time, then zig zag my way back to the car. I was just getting ready to turn around when the shoes busted open a blister on my heel. Every step became searing, burning agony. Not one to waste an opportunity, I wasn't about to just walk straight back to the car without completing my mission of canvassing the other side of the street. I steeled my nerves against the pain and reaffirmed my commitment. For the next hour, I hobbled up front steps to people's doors, smiled through the inferno of pain in my foot, and introduced myself again and again. Finally, I made it back to the car and reached into the glove box to fish out the ancient first aid kit that I'd assembled as a boy scout project a decade earlier. There were exactly two band aids left, which I carefully layered over the blister to give enough padding to finish the final two hours of canvassing that day.

Arriving back home that evening, I was fed up with my dress-shoe get up. What was the point of subjecting myself to the torture of sweat and blisters if everyone still thought I looked too young to fit their preconceived notions of what a "mayor" was anyway? I threw the shoes away and promised myself that I would embrace more comfortable attire, because I had too much ground to cover to let a pair of uncomfortable shoes hold me back.

A Sense of Belonging

"Now, the energy is more around the idea that the cities that succeed are the ones that allow people to help create them. That's how they become better places, but also how people are going to become more attached to them. When people help create their place, they see themselves reflected in it. It reflects their values and personalities and becomes more an extension of themselves.

Ethan Kent

Louise and her husband moved to Burlington after they retired from their respective careers, seeking a quiet place to live out their years together. Unfortunately, shortly after moving to the community, Louise's husband passed away. After a decades-long marriage, Louise found herself entirely alone, lacking either family or friends nearby. With very few relationships and at a loss as to how to connect with the community, Louise spent the next several years in isolating loneliness.

I met Louise while canvassing her neighborhood. We sat on a small wooden bench that decorated her raised concrete stoop and talked for the better part of an hour. As we talked, I pondered the question, what is it that inspires people to connect with their community? How many people wish they could find something that pulls them out of their loneliness and into something bigger than themselves, but they're never able to find it because they don't know where to look? How many missed opportunities are out there because we lack a way to connect people?

For Louise, the opportunity came via a chance meeting. A local pastor lived a few blocks down her street and they happened to meet one day as he walked past her house. He invited her to visit his church, which was her first invitation to connect with the community, years after she arrived. The relationship she now has with the members of that organization give her a reason to call Burlington home. She passionately loves her community and enjoys a new sense of belonging where before there was only loneliness. This entire change in her life occurred because one person was willing to reach out and invite her to connect.

Everyone deserves to feel like they belong in their community, and Burlington is stronger with every connection. When people feel like they are part of something bigger than themselves, their passion is infectious. They unlock their potential and reach out to others to pull them up too. A sense of community can be a lifeline out of the dark. It can be your support network when you meet a challenge and your celebration when you succeed. It can be the mentorship that our children need to follow their dreams. It can be the opportunity to improve the quality of life of your loved ones.

It was for this reason that one of my first projects after I was elected Mayor in 2015 was developing a program to welcome new residents to Burlington. The program, which we've named Belong in Burlington, is a free quarterly event that is designed to connect new residents to opportunities within the city. From the very beginning, I wanted this program to be about relationships. After all, Louise didn't find her place in our community because someone handed her a flyer. Belong in Burlington provides the opportunity to meet the Mayor, City Council members, city manager, police chief, fire chief, library services director, animal services director, United Way director, representatives from Alamance Community College, members of the downtown Makerspace, and other new residents in the community.

Belong in Burlington is about building personal relationships with people who share your interests. If you loved volunteering with your local animal shelter previously, you can meet the people who will be volunteering alongside you if you choose to volunteer with our animal shelter. If you're interested in public safety, we can connect you with our Citizen's Police Academy or introduce you to members of our fire department. If you have kids and you're looking for activities to entertain them after school or over summer break, you can shake hands with the people who would be caring for them. Whether you're looking for ways to get involved, recreational activities, health services, ways to get around, or educational opportunities for yourself or your children, Belong in Burlington can introduce you to a person that can serve as your way to get plugged-in locally.

Some of my favorite conversations along the campaign trail were with new residents. As they answered the door I'd greet them with a smile and a hearty welcome. From there I'd learn all about their journey and what drew them to our community. Today, I get to have those same conversations as I welcome them to our City Hall and invite them to call Burlington home.

An Invitation to Engage

"Leaders can conceive and articulate goals that lift people out of their petty preoccupations and carry them above the conflicts that tear a society apart."

John W Gardner

Having learned my lesson with my first pair of dress shoes, I made sure my next pair was well broken-in. My moderately-worn pair of brown, outlet-store Oxfords were very similar to that now-discarded pair of black shoes, but for some reason they had always been much more forgiving on my feet. At the same time, I abandoned the formality of canvassing in a full suit in exchange for dress slacks and a button-down shirt, often with the sleeves rolled neatly to my elbows.

With my lightened attire, I found sprinting up front steps much easier. The August heat gave way to milder September days, which made my long hours outdoors much more enjoyable. I'd begun to find my rhythm too. On weekdays, I knew that the best canvassing hours were from mid-afternoon until dusk, which left my mornings available to attend to my product manufacturing and design company. Weekends were golden, and every hour of daylight was a precious opportunity to pound the pavement.

To get the most out of a full day of canvassing, I carefully prepared the evening before. Water bottles filled my freezer so they'd be frozen by the morning. I'd load up my green hatchback with yard signs to place throughout the day. The front passenger seat was transformed into a well-organized collection of campaign materials, complete with informational walk cards, voter registration forms, early-voting pamphlets, rubber bands with clothespins to secure walk cards to front doors, and plenty of extra pens. The foot wells were littered with granola bars and a few other snacks to be enjoyed in the brief breaks I had between neighborhoods. A raincoat was always tucked behind the seat, ready for inevitable drippy days.

The whole process became a dance. I'd drive to a neighborhood and search for a nice shady spot to park the car. Then I'd grab my clipboard, a handful of flyers, fill my pockets with rubber bands, and begin hopping from house to house and block to block. When I'd done a full lap of the surrounding few blocks, I'd return to the car for a quick drive down a few more streets to start it all again. More than a few times, my hybrid car got to the point where it struggled to start as the battery strained from too few miles of driving to keep it charged. All the while, I kept a stack of notes compiling each topic that residents brought up and tied the issues back to the exact neighborhoods where they were most relevant or pressing.

During this same time, my conversations with voters started to result in book recommendations. Standing on their front porch, talking about the lack of sidewalks, the need for safe places for kids to play, or overflowing storm drains, they would be reminded of a book that they recently read. The conversation would shift to the suggestion that I read the book in my spare time. Spare time is not something that exists for candidates during election season, so those books joined an ever-growing "to read" list.

Prior to the election, I'd been an avid reader. Non-fiction captured my engineering mind as I jumped between all manner of subjects. Some of the highlights were <u>The Box: How the Shipping Container Make the World Smaller and the World Economy Bigger</u> by Marc Levinson and <u>The Big Roads: The Untold Story of the Engineers, Visionaries, and Trailblazers Who Created the American Superhighways</u> by Earl Swift. I loved exploring the deeper forces that influence our world and the power that a strong, well implemented vision can have on the future of our society. Implementation was always a key theme. Without gaining buy-in from a community, even the best ideas will languish on the forgotten dusty shelves of history.

It was in this period that I met Thomas. I knocked on his door around mid-afternoon on one of those long weekend days. My legs were weary from the endless hours of walking, and those trusty brown Oxfords were beginning to give way at the seams. On Thomas' shaded front porch, I lingered a little longer than usual, and we spent more than the normal few minutes chatting. Our conversation included a range of topics, suggestions, and questions, and before long it turned to a book recommendation. However, unlike those before it, this recommendation came with an invitation to resume the discussion later, once I finally found the time to read the book.

That small suggestion planted a seed of an idea that grew as I walked onward. Certainly, each book I read alone would offer the opportunity to understand a new perspective, but the impact of that same book could be compounded if a team of readers was willing and able to put their own effort behind enacting the lessons learned. By exploring a text through many people's individual lenses of human experience, we could find a more complete understanding of the impact of the concepts on our local community. A new idea for engaging the readers of our city started to take shape.

That idea would finally mature during my 2015 mayoral race. By that time, the list of books had grown to over 50 titles. I resolved that win or lose, after that campaign I would make more time to put a dent in that list. With our campaign win that November, I unleashed the floodgates of pent-up pages and we kicked off what is now known as the Mayor's Book Club. This initiative tackles a different text each month and invites the whole city to gather, discuss, and apply the concepts to our community. To my knowledge, our program is the only one in the country in which the Mayor actively participates in the book club discussions.

Many of those books are heavy in both pages and content, but we continue to gain new readers from across our city each month. To make the club accessible and inviting to a broad range of readers, we rotate the location of discussions between the traditional library setting, local restaurants, and a few local bars for good measure. Each month we welcome new readers who stumble upon the group and together with open minds we tackle the hard task of reshaping these lofty concepts into actionable ideas that fit the unique flavor of the Burlington community.

I'm sad to say that those poor worn shoes didn't live to see the book club take life. Early in the 2014 campaign season, they began to take a turn for the worst as the miles took their toll. The leather cracked and split, enabling onlookers to easily tell what color socks I'd chosen to wear that day. Rain poured in and soaked my feet. By October of that year, they had been retired and a new pair took their place. Their service is remembered via the people and places they carried me in my perpetual mission for expanded community engagement.

Innovation and Opportunity

"As for the future, your task is not to foresee it,
but to enable it."

Antoine de Saint-Exupery

I am an entrepreneur. As the co-owner of Vibration Solution, LLC, I am frequently on the phone with customers to help them problem-solve the best way to use our products to accomplish their goal. These engineering conversations can range from simple home audio installations to more complex isolation of nanosatellites being blasted into orbit. This entrepreneurial, problem-solving spirit drives everything I do, all the way down to my shoes. Although the brown Oxfords struggled their way through the end of the 2013 campaign, by the 2014 race for North Carolina State House District 63, I needed my third pair of campaigning shoes. I found a pair of grey cloth slip-ons that were comfortable from the first moment I wore them. About half way through the campaign season, we had a series of particularly wet, rainy days and, much to my confusion, I found that every time I got back in my car, a small portion of my right sock, near the heel, was wet. The uppers were still dry, and the left sock was fine as well.

The inner soles of these shoes were not solid, and instead their rubber was molded into a hollow waffle pattern. Upon close inspection, I discovered that the bottom of the right heel had worn through an area in the thin portion of the waffle; just enough so water would seep into the insole every time I stepped in a puddle. Frustrated and short on time to buy new shoes, I found some Shoe Goo epoxy and used it to fill in the waffle pattern so the shoe would be water-tight again. I successfully made it through the rest of that election season with dry socks.

Problem solving comes naturally to me. If there's a problem, I evaluate the resources available to me and make the best decision I can based on the information before me. This served me well when we were struggling to find ways to energize the creativity of our community and channel that energy to captivate people's imagination. Simply put, we were looking for ideas to add "wow" factor to our community.

The answer came, as most entrepreneurial solutions do, from a combination of unique resources and lucky timing. It began with reading <u>Love Where You Live: Creating Emotionally Engaging Places</u> by Peter Kageyama. I was drawn to the book because it features a wealth of real-world examples of citizens taking matters into their own hands and reinventing the places that they live. The author devoted one section of the book to a unique local grant program called The Awesome Foundation. Unlike most traditional grants, which require pages and pages of applications, essays, forms, and endorsements, The Awesome Foundation focuses on the person and their idea. There are no minimum word counts, and the grant is awarded in the form of a bag of cash with no strings attached. It is a gift that is given in good faith with trust and hope that the grantee will go on to complete their proposed project.

Awesome Foundations are formed when ten or more people come together and each chip in one hundred dollars. They then call for people from across the community to pitch their ideas for a project. In the book, Peter uses the example of a 40-person hammock that was constructed in a park in his hometown of St. Petersburg, Florida. I loved the idea of the community coming together to support a project that seems so ridiculously out-there and abnormal that no other government or community entity would support it.

Just a few months later, I had the opportunity to visit St. Petersburg while participating in the Kauffman Foundation Mayors' Conference on Entrepreneurship. Mayor Rick Kriseman of St. Petersburg was an active part of the conference, and I had time to talk with him about Peter Kageyama and the impact of creative placemaking strategies like The Awesome Foundation. Upon returning to Burlington, I sat down to debrief ideas with a loosely formed new board dedicated to gathering local entrepreneurs and directing their efforts towards community growth and development. During the meeting, I briefly mentioned some of the projects, while not mentioning the fund by name. Jason Cox, founder of Co|Operative in Graham paused and asked, "Are those related to The Awesome Foundation?" After that, the spark was lit.

At our first Engage Alamance entrepreneurship session, I tossed the idea to the crowd of sixty-some innovators and extended the invitation that anyone interested in contributing one hundred dollars should talk to me afterwards. By the end of the week, our first Awesome Foundation grant had been formed, and just three months later we would award our first bag of cash. The winner was Charlotte Wray, a young journalist with a passion for pollinators. Her application stood out above the other sixteen because she recognized the grant for what it was intended to be: a catalyst for greater things. She pitched the idea of creating a series of local pollinator gardens around our county and using those gardens to educate the public about the critical role of pollinators in production of our food. Furthermore, she wanted to create a website to promote local awareness and ultimately build partnerships with local agencies so our community could earn "Bee City USA" status. We felt this was an AWESOME use of the grant!

Within just a few months, Charlotte had selected the garden sites, launched her website, and was well on her way to make Pollinate Alamance a reality. It's exactly this hands-on, direct, action-oriented attitude that makes entrepreneurs and community innovators successful. When a problem strikes, look around, take stock of what you've got, and give it a shot. Sometimes we fail, but failure is an opportunity to learn, refine, and retry.

The Shoe Goo fix was a success and those grey slip-ons lasted well into 2015. Unfortunately, more and more of the hollow waffle soles wore through, and they started to take on water in even the lightest drizzle. Eventually, the soles were more Shoe Goo than rubber, so I retired the shoes from their hard life on the campaign trail. The 2014 campaign was a tough loss, and I took an eight-month-long break from politics while I recovered both mentally and financially. Nevertheless, I found myself filing to run for Mayor again in the summer of 2015, and this time would prove to be different.

Having a Beer with the Mayor

"If you had to choose between 10 percent more cops on the beat or 10 percent more citizens knowing their neighbors' first names, the latter is a better crime prevention strategy."

*Seguaro Seminar,
Harvard's Kennedy School of Government*

By the time the third pair of shoes was wearing out, I had identified a specific list of ideal features found in a good pair of canvassing shoes. At the top of the list, accented in bold with a dozen underlines and stars, was comfort. Second on the list was easy to tie or slip on and off. Sadly, that eliminated my whole collection of Converse Chuck Taylor Hi-Tops. However, my next-most readily-available pair of shoes was a pair of recently-retired running shoes. They had served me well for a few seasons of running, and together we'd completed numerous 5k races, 10k races, and a muddy 14-mile trail run the previous December. After a few cycles in the washing machine, they were clean enough for the campaign trail.

Compared to my first campaign years, my attire now ranked as exceedingly casual. Along the way, as I shed layers of formality, I feared that people would consider me less and less viable of a candidate for Mayor. What I found was that while the questions and jokes about my young age continued, each interaction proceeded in a similar pattern. On each doorstep, porch, and driveway, as the minutes passed and the conversation deepened, people came to realize that the interaction they had with me was more important than my specific age or attire. This was the first time that many of them had ever met a candidate for elected office, let alone had the opportunity to directly share their thoughts, feelings, opinions, and suggestions.

The purpose of my shoes was not to convey a tone of professionalism or status. Instead, it was to physically convey me to the people I sought to represent. With those somewhat-faded, blue-and-yellow running shoes, I found the steps, blocks, and miles melt away easily beneath my feet. They made it a joy to sprint up each set of stairs. That was the critical element, because every door, no matter if it was the first or the last of each day, was a specific, singular opportunity to build a relationship, share in someone's perspective on the world, and further my own understanding of the diverse challenges facing our city. If I let my aching muscles dictate my enthusiasm for the task at hand, each conversation would have become less and less productive.

We canvassed right up until the polls closed on November 3, 2015. On Election Day, I awoke early, well before the polls opened at 6:30am. As the sun rose and our volunteers fanned out across the city to each of the polling stations, I prepared to make the final canvassing push. Together with Mike, one of our amazing volunteers, I planned to smash our daily record for door-knocking. Starting at 9am, wearing my normal attire of a button-up shirt, dark jeans, beat up running shoes, and my oversized green and blue "Ian Baltutis for Mayor" badge, I climbed into the passenger seat of Mike's truck to begin the marathon.

Most candidates choose to work the polls on Election Day, which usually means selecting one of a dozen polling locations, and then spending the day handing out pens, info cards, or campaign-branded emery boards to everyone who shows up to vote. I preferred a different strategy, which was to keep canvassing until the final minutes of the election. For most people, by the time they have resolved to get in their car and go vote, they have already decided which candidate they will support. If you haven't made up your mind by Election Day, odds are you'll decide to sit the election out entirely. We were still focused on our original goal of increasing community involvement, so we were not satisfied with the usual politics and low voter turnout. We wanted to see more people engaged, excited, and participating in the election.

Thus, the marathon began. Mike would drop me off at one end of a block and I would proceed to run up to each house, knock, wait, leave a note reminding them of the election, and then sprint onward to the next house. When I reached the end of the street, I jumped back into the truck and headed to the next group of houses. For those who were home that Tuesday, I had the opportunity to make my final pleas for support in hopes of earning a few more votes. After having lost the two previous elections, I took nothing for granted. Small-time municipal races do not have polling data to give an indication of how the election might turn out. We had to use every precious moment in hopes that it was enough to push us over the edge to victory.

The race continued, hour by hour, through clouds and drizzle. By mid-afternoon, more and more of the people answering the door were proudly sporting their "I Voted" stickers. Many of them greeted me with a smile, encouraging words, and appreciation for our efforts as they spurred me onward. Aside from a brief lunch break at one of my favorite taquerias, Mike and I continued at a blistering pace. As the sun began to dip closer to the horizon, we pushed even harder. We'd park the truck at the end of a street and then divide and conquer with Mike taking one side of the street and I the other. When the sun finally dipped below the trees and the twilight became too dark to read addresses on the houses, we stopped. The final tally of doors for the day had just surpassed seven hundred, which was a new personal record. We headed to the nearest voting poll and spent the final hour greeting some of the same people who we'd met just moments earlier on their doorsteps. When the clock finally struck 7:30pm, with tired bodies, sore muscles, and weary eyes, we knew that we had done our best.

In high school, I had a cross country running coach who would admonish us to "leave it all on the course." She would raise all hell and fury if we crossed the finish line with a smile, as she felt that meant we hadn't poured ourselves totally and completely into the race. As Mike and I drove back to campaign headquarters, the exhaustion I felt was mirrored by satisfaction in having worked hard for a worthy cause. I could still manage a smile, but just barely, as I changed out of those now sweaty, sticky clothes, and very well-worn shoes.

The election party was a short drive from my house. As Kristina and I drove there, the early voting results were released. After pulling them up on her phone, she turned to me as we drove and asked if I wanted to know the initial results. In our two previous races, the results had started bad and only gotten worse, so it was with a deep hesitation that I consented to hear the early numbers. My worry was short-lived. The results of early voting showed us nearly ten percentage points ahead. Upon arriving at the party, our supporters erupted into cheers and congratulations. As the minutes ticked by, we shared stories of the campaign, nursed our beers, and awaited the final results.

I've often heard folks refer to approachable politicians as "someone you could have a beer with." There we stood, in a local pizzeria, hosting a campaign after-party with no guest list. Anyone who wanted to join us was welcome. With friends both new and old, we gathered to celebrate a new chapter for our community. I have a vision where this camaraderie of the campaign trail might someday be the normal relationship between citizens and elected leaders. It was there that we watched our years of hard work pay off as the final results came in showing that Burlington had just elected its youngest Mayor in the history of the community.

Making A Difference at Any Age

"If all mankind minus one were of one opinion, and only one person were of contrary opinion, mankind would be no more justified in silencing that one person than he, if he had the power, would be justified in silencing mankind."

John Stuart Mill

Shortly after I was elected Mayor in 2015, I reached out to connect with our local schools. I immensely value the opportunity to challenge students to get involved and offer their unique perspective on the future of our community. A few weeks after extending this challenge to a fourth-grade classroom, I received an email from a student named Anna. She shared her passion for skateboarding, which is her preferred way to stay fit, connect with her community, and have fun. She then went on to explain that she is frustrated that skateboarding is not legal in Burlington. She asked what could be done to help law-abiding people like her enjoy this activity legally.

When I first read her email, I was shocked. Surely, she must have misinterpreted the rules. But sure enough, I discovered after a bit of research that she was right. In Burlington, we have strict city ordinances in place which limit skateboarding to the extent that it is effectively illegal. You are not allowed to skateboard on the street anywhere in the city or on any sidewalk in the main downtown area. Because we've historically invested very little in expanding our sidewalk network, the locations where one can legally and safely skateboard are very limited and poorly connected.

I kept investigating. How many other people share this sentiment? What amenities are available to skateboarders now? Why do these ordinances exist in the first place? Before long, it became obvious that the best way to find out more was to reach out and have a conversation with the wider skateboarding community. After all, I'm not a skateboarder myself, so it would be impractical for me to believe that I could fully grasp the entirety of the situation from the outside.

I invited Burlington's skateboarding community to join me for a discussion at the Historic Train Depot. It's hard to get people to show up to city-government-sponsored events, but on that evening the Depot was filled to standing room only. Over 100 people showed up to share their passion for skateboarding and to talk about the future of skateboarding in our community. This group included folks of all ages and walks of life. Pastors, lawyers, college students, and business professionals all piled into the cramped room to share how skateboarding impacted their lives. These stories introduced me to a community within Burlington about which I had previously known very little.

Students shared that the friends they developed while skateboarding improved their perspective on diversity because skateboarding brought together people from different cultures, languages, and socioeconomic backgrounds. Skateboarding was the students' opportunity to reach outside their peer group and build connections with these people. Business professionals shared that skateboarding was an important part of their development as individuals, and that it helped to shape them into the people they are today. Some still skateboard occasionally, and while they aren't likely to try the daredevil moves of their past, they would still appreciate having a place to practice their tamer tricks.

Despite my research, no one can give me a clear answer on why our ordinances regarding skateboarding are so strict. Most cities ban skateboarding in places where it is unsafe, such as busy roads and areas with heavy pedestrian traffic. Burlington may have tried to enact a similar policy, restricting skateboarding only to sidewalks in residential neighborhoods, but without considering that we've invested very little in residential sidewalk infrastructure.

We are still looking for support from City Council to relax the rules on skateboarding and expand the opportunity for this form of recreation and transit. However, if it weren't for Anna's email, we wouldn't have had a community skateboarding forum, and we wouldn't have started this wider discussion in a more formal manner. Now that we have, we are working to make a difference. We're trying to change the ordinances to be more supportive of skateboarding, and we've even discussed the possibility of a skate park down the road.

Anna's story illustrates how important it is for people to share their perspective with me. While people joke about me being everywhere, no single person, myself included, will ever be able to experience each facet of what makes Burlington a place worth living for all her residents. Anna was in fourth grade when she sent her email, which illustrates that you are never too young, or too old, to make a difference. You have a unique perspective that I don't have, and sharing that helps me tremendously as we strive to make Burlington the best it can be.

The Strength of a Connected Community

*Planning of the automobile city focuses on saving time.
Planning for the accessible city, on the other hand, focuses
on time well spent.*

Robert Cervero

When I first started canvassing in 2013, door after door after door, I asked people what issues were important to them, and the overwhelming response was public transportation. City Council had started discussions about implementing a bus system, but it had been a very low priority item, so conversations had dragged out for nearly seven years, and there was no clear public timeline for when it would exist.

Because it was clear to me from my door-to-door conversations that the clear majority of citizens supported action on a public transportation system, this issue became one of the cornerstones of my campaign platform. By doing this, I could affect the conversation surrounding the election, and by the end of that election season, every candidate for both City Council and Mayor had taken a positive stance on public transit. Even though I lost the

2013 election, the amount of community engagement on this topic put pressure on City Council to prioritize plans for transit. In April 2014, the council approved a timeline for Link Transit, with service slated to being in summer 2016. Whereas the plan had previously been gathering dust for nearly seven years, it took only 5 months to gain approval after the community banded together to offer their voices in support.

Therefore, it was in June 2016, after I had been elected Mayor in November 2015, when the Link Transit system finally launched. The morning of the launch, I was scheduled to give a talk at Alamance Community College's Dillingham Campus, so I got up early, bicycled down to the nearest stop, caught the very first Blue Route bus from near my house, and then transferred to the Orange Route out from the hub. It was so early that the ACC Dillingham campus wasn't open yet. I could have left the bus at my intended stop and waited until the campus opened, but I was having a nice chat with the bus driver, so I decided to ride the bus all the way out to Alamance Community College's Main Campus and then back to the Dillingham Campus, since I had the time anyway.

When we arrived at the Alamance Community College Main Campus stop, a single rider boarded. I introduced myself as the Mayor and welcomed him to the bus. His name was Nathan, and he shared that he was excited the Link Transit system was finally in place, because he was planning on riding it to work. As we continued our conversation, I learned that Nathan worked at the Steak N Shake on Huffman Mill Rd, and every day up until now, Nathan didn't have a consistent way to get to work. Sometimes he could bum rides with friends, but that often only worked one way and not the other. In that situation, he would walk home, which took about two hours one way. Several days a week, he walked both to and from work, for a total of four hours spent on his commute that day.

He was excited for Link Transit because it meant he would have a reliable method of transportation to work, enabling him to rely less on his friends and coworkers. Even though he had to take the Orange Line all the way to the hub and then transfer to the Red Line, taking the bus would save him approximately 45 minutes of transit time both to and from work. This would enable him to get more sleep, making him more alert at work, and would also enable him to spend more time with his children in the evenings.

When we sketched out the routes for Link Transit, we assumed that the Orange Line would serve students attending Alamance Community College, but here was a person who now has a better quality of life because he was able to ride the bus. Critics of the bus system always want to know when the system is going to break even. I would challenge them to include in their calculations the improvement to Nathan's children's lives because their father is around to help them with homework in the evenings, the increased productivity Nathan's employer enjoys because Nathan is a better employee when he's well-rested, and the benefit to our society for not having to pay unemployment if Nathan were to lose his job from missing too many days of work because of unreliable transportation.

When I finally did arrive at the Dillingham Campus for my talk, I had an incredible story to tell about the impact our bus system was already having on its very first day. Now that we have over a year of data to review, I feel strongly that our public transit system should continue to expand. Additional buses, later hours, and buses running on weekends would be a huge asset to our community, and would help people like Nathan be happy, healthy, productive members of our wonderful city.

I have the luxury of owning and driving a car. But I still take time to ride Link Transit and speak with the riders. Each time that I ride, I meet more and more people with similarly-compelling stories. Whether it's someone who can visit a loved one in the hospital, a senior citizen who can run their own errands, or a student attending classes, all these riders share a similar theme. Riding Link Transit provides them the freedom to access, interact with, and contribute to our city. It is their doorway to opportunity and liberty. Their lives become better every day that they board our bright, clean, green and blue buses.

Conclusion

"A place belongs forever to whomever claims it hardest, remembers it most obsessively, wrenches it from itself, shapes it, renders it, loves it so radically that he remakes it in his own image."

Joan Didion

At no point prior to 2013 did I aspire to pursue elected office. It was never on my radar, my aspirational goal list, or my bucket list. But on that day in July of 2013 when I received that phone call, my life, my priorities, and my role in the community changed forever. Those three hard campaigns, the blisters, the rainy days, the sore feet, and the long nights have all been part of an amazing journey. Looking back, I would not trade those experiences for anything.

If you had to place a bet on the introverted engineer from Minnesota becoming the youngest Mayor in Burlington's history, you would have been smart to put your money elsewhere. But through a lot of long days, with the help and advice of friends, family, and, most importantly, the people of Burlington, something amazing happened. I plunged headfirst into our community and found myself

warmly received as its new-found champion. The
Christmas after the 2013 Election, my brother gave me a
book, The Metropolitan Revolution by Bruce Katz and
Jennifer Bradley. There is a passage in the book from the
Plain Dealer newspaper that has stuck with me:

> *No mayor, however persuasive or dynamic, is
> unilaterally going to transform the [region]. No lone-
> eagle innovator, however ingenious, instantly will
> reverse decades of income stagnation and educational
> neglect. No single public project, however daring, will
> make this region a magnet for the smart, industrious
> people who are the raw material of the Information
> Age. Instead, lots of people, acting individually and
> collectively in different arenas and different niches,
> must step up and lead.*

If you ask a child what powers a mayor has (as I often do
when I visit schools), they will often rank them on par
with Superman. However, we are mere mortals, as frail, as
flawed, and as human as every single other resident of our
community. The only difference is that we have a
megaphone and pulpit from which to rally the citizens. We
have a unique vantage point from which to become the
champion of our amazing fellow humans who also call this
city home. It is how we leverage this wonderful pulpit that
defines how effectively we mobilize all our neighbors
about the task of remaking our city.

To effectively mobilize a community, you must begin with
a vision to unify its citizens. For me, that vision was
written by the previous City Council in our Destination
Burlington Strategic Plan, which was adopted only months
before I took office. It laid out a vision for a modern,
vibrant city, designed for people at human scale. It
proposed solutions sourced from our citizens to bridge
divides and unite our city both emotionally and physically.

Like so many previous plans, it risked being doomed to a dark shelf where it would collect dust and fade from memory. In my first term as Mayor, we have made that plan our guiding vision and asked each community organization to unite in support of it. Together, we are finally pulling together, in a unified direction.

The process is slow, but it's getting faster. Our city is building momentum as more people are coming together and each finding their own way to give back. On the tough days, the slow days, the days where it seems like no progress is being made, I take a moment to reflect. As citizens, as residents, we become accustomed and comfortable in our community. We become blind to the wonderful things around us as we busy ourselves with our daily tasks. However, when we host a visitor or show a family member around our city, we see our community anew through the eyes of an outsider. It reawakens us to the wonderful place that is Burlington. Taking a brief break to remind myself of the way our city looks to an outsider invigorates me onward.

If that doesn't lift my spirits, I have a whole set of shelves in my office at City Hall covered with letters that people have sent me along this journey. Some letters are formal, and others are written in crayon on construction paper. Each note reminds me of an interaction along my journey. Those kind words of encouragement re-energize me about the task of pushing onward. Forging ahead and exploring new trails is exhausting, but endlessly rewarding.

There will always be more work to do. The role of Mayor has no instruction manual, no guide, and no cheat sheet. I can only hope that the work we do today better prepares the leaders of tomorrow to succeed. I hope that the students I inspire on my next classroom visit will someday take up the mantle of public service and carry on, each generation remaking our city. For now, it is my honor to serve as we strive to build a city filled with diverse neighborhoods, active parks, and a vibrant downtown, brimming with multiple generations of citizens who love calling this place, this Burlington, home.

About the Author

Mayor Ian Baltutis, elected in 2015, is a 2008 Business Entrepreneurship graduate of Elon University. He has worked for businesses both large and small in roles that include customer service, technology support, logistics, and management. Currently, he owns and manages Vibration Solution LLC, an American product design and manufacturing company that he founded during his studies at Elon. His company competes on a global scale while continuing to create local jobs. He regularly lectures to students and business professionals of all ages around the country about innovation, the future of international business, the Maker Movement, careers for social good, and the power of the Internet.

Baltutis is an Eagle Scout who believes in always giving back to his community through service, leadership, and philanthropy. In his free time, he tutors elementary math and science, volunteers with Elon University, advises start-up entrepreneurs, and mentors youth through the local Boy Scout Venture program. Baltutis enjoys tinkering in the garage, and his project for the last 10 years has been the careful restoration of a 1974 MGB GT Pepsi Pace Car that he found in a barn in Minnesota. He also loves maintaining his daily driver, a unique lime green 2000 Honda Insight hybrid. He loves the open road and exploring the United States on our nation's backroads and historic highways.

His other hobbies include wood working, brewing beer, and hiking with his partner, Kristina, and their dogs. Ian and Kristina can often be spotted bicycling around the Burlington community.